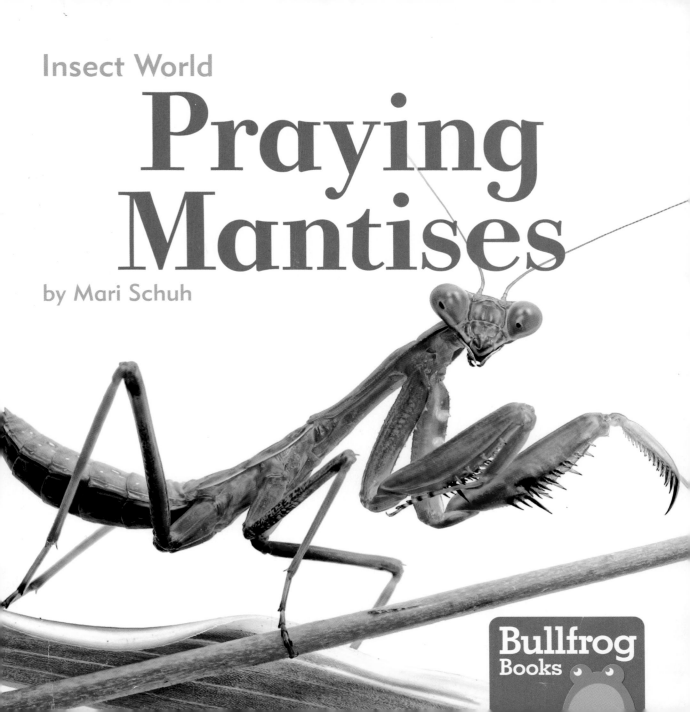

Insect World

Praying Mantises

by Mari Schuh

Bullfrog Books

Ideas for Parents and Teachers

Bullfrog Books let children practice reading informational text at the earliest reading levels. Repetition, familiar words, and photo labels support early readers.

Before Reading

- Discuss the cover photo. What does it tell them?

- Look at the picture glossary together. Read and discuss the words.

Read the Book

- "Walk" through the book and look at the photos. Let the child ask questions. Point out the photo labels.

- Read the book to the child, or have him or her read independently.

After Reading

- Prompt the child to think more. Ask: Have you ever seen a praying mantis? What was it doing? Where do you think you would see one?

The author dedicates this book to Jake Quam.

Bullfrog Books are published by Jump!
5357 Penn Avenue South
Minneapolis, MN 55419
www.jumplibrary.com

Library of Congress Cataloging-in-Publication Data

Schuh, Mari C., 1975– author.
  Praying mantises / by Mari Schuh.
    pages cm. — (Insect world)
  Audience: Age 5.
  Audience: K to grade 3.
  Includes index.
  ISBN 978-1-62031-163-9 (hardcover) —
  ISBN 978-1-62496-250-9 (ebook)
  1. Praying mantis—Juvenile literature. I. Title. II. Series: Schuh, Mari C., 1975– Insect world.
  QL505.9.M35S38 2015
  595.7'27 — dc23
                                    2014032116

Series Editor: Rebecca Glaser
Series Designer: Ellen Huber
Book Designer: Anna Peterson
Photo Researcher: Jenny Fretland VanVoorst

Photo Credits: All photos by Shutterstock except: Dreamstime, 16–17, 19, 23bl, 23br; National Geographic Creative, 14–15; SuperStock, 5; Thinkstock, 20–21, 23tl.

Printed in the United States of America at Corporate Graphics, in North Mankato, Minnesota.

Table of Contents

Hungry Hunters

A praying mantis hides.

It waits for its prey.

It is hard to see.

It is green like the leaves.

It folds its front legs.
It is ready to hunt.

It turns its head.

Big eyes look for bugs to eat.

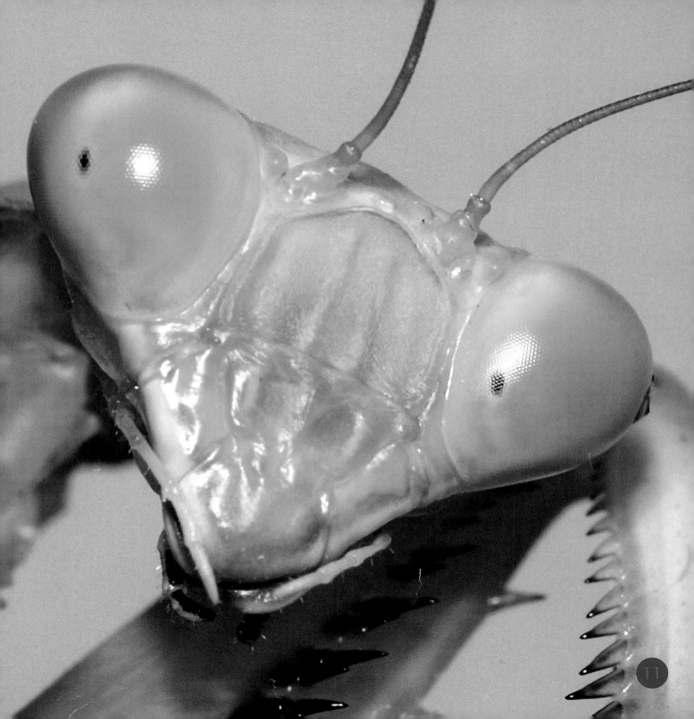

Oh, no!
A bird is here.

12

The mantis stands up.

13

It fans out its wings.

It looks big.

The bird flies away.

Look!

A bug lands nearby.

The mantis strikes!

It grabs the bug.

Spines on its legs hold the bug.

spine ····▶

The mantis eats and eats.

It grooms its legs
and head.

Now it is clean.

It is ready for
its next meal.

Parts of a Praying Mantis

antennas
A praying mantis smells and feels with two thin antennas.

eyes
Big eyes help praying mantises find prey.

wings
Many praying mantises have wings.

front legs
Praying mantises fold their front legs. It looks like they are praying.

Picture Glossary

groom
To take care of and to clean.

spine
A pointy, sharp part on an insect's body.

prey
Insects and animals that are hunted for food.

strike
To hit or attack; praying mantises quickly strike their prey.

Index

To Learn More

Learning more is as easy as 1, 2, 3.

1) Go to www.factsurfer.com

2) Enter "praying mantises" into the search box.

3) Click the "Surf" button to see a list of websites.

With factsurfer.com, finding more information is just a click away.